Team Spirit®

THE NEW JERSEY NETS

BY

MARK STEWART

Content Consultant
Matt Zeysing
Historian and Archivist
The Naismith Memorial Basketball Hall of Fame

NORWOOD HOUSE PRESS

CHICAGO, ILLINOIS

Norwood House Press
P.O. Box 316598
Chicago, Illinois 60631

For information regarding Norwood House Press, please visit our website at:
www.norwoodhousepress.com or call 866-565-2900.

All photos courtesy of Getty Images except the following:
The New York Nets (6), Topps, Inc. (7, 14, 16, 20, 34 both, 36, 38, 40 top & bottom left, 41 all),
Associated Press (17, 18), Black Book Partners (19), The Star Co. (21 bottom, 35 top left, 43),
Author's Collection (35 top right), Matt Richman (48)
Cover photo: Bill Kostroun/Associated Press
Special thanks to Topps, Inc.

Editor: Mike Kennedy
Designer: Ron Jaffe
Project Management: Black Book Partners, LLC.
Research: Joshua Zaffos
Special thanks to Fred King and Keith Young

Library of Congress Cataloging-in-Publication Data

Stewart, Mark, 1960-
  The New Jersey Nets / by Mark Stewart ; content consultant, Matt Zeysing.
    p. cm. -- (Team spirit)
  Summary: "Presents the history, accomplishments, and key personalities of
the New Jersey Nets basketball team. Includes timelines, quotes, maps,
glossary and website"--Provided by publisher.
  Includes bibliographical references and index.
  ISBN-13: 978-1-59953-124-3 (library edition : alk. paper)
  ISBN-10: 1-59953-124-0 (library edition : alk. paper) 1. New Jersey Nets
(Basketball team)--History--Juvenile literature. I. Zeysing, Matt. II.
Title.
  GV885.52.N37S74 2009
  796.323'640974921--dc22
                                              2007011707

Manufactured in the United States of America.

COVER PHOTO: The Nets celebrate a victory during the 2008–09 season.

Table of Contents

SPORTS WORDS & VOCABULARY WORDS: In this book, you will find many words that are new to you. You may also see familiar words used in new ways. The glossary on page 46 gives the meanings of basketball words, as well as "everyday" words that have special basketball meanings. These words appear in **bold type** throughout the book. The glossary on page 47 gives the meanings of vocabulary words that are not related to basketball. They appear in ***bold italic type*** throughout the book.

BASKETBALL SEASONS: Because each basketball season begins late in one year and ends early in the next, seasons are not named after years. Instead, they are written out as two years separated by a dash, for example 1944–45 or 2005–06.

Meet the Nets

Every basketball team needs a leader. This player does not have to be the tallest, fastest, strongest, or even the team's star. He simply needs to know how to make his teammates play better. The New Jersey Nets are proof of this. They have had many great players over the years. Yet the team has only been a winner when a true leader has stepped forward.

The Nets are very good at building around these special leaders. They look for players with different skills, *upbeat* attitudes, and a deep desire to win. Some are stars and some are **substitutes**. All have something positive to offer.

This book tells the story of the Nets. They have soared, and they have struggled. At all times, however, they have put up a great fight. When you play for the Nets, there is only one rule—never stop looking for ways to win and never be satisfied until you do.

Devin Harris welcomes teammate Yi Jianlian onto the floor during a 2008–09 game.

Way Back When

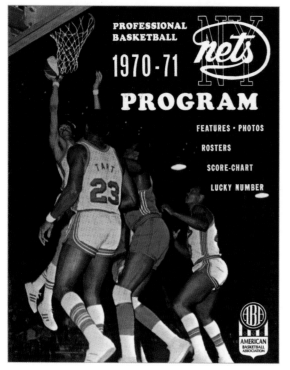

In 1967, the **American Basketball Association (ABA)** began its first season. The ABA wanted to put a team in New York City. The league hoped to use an old *armory* on the East Side of Manhattan as the club's home court. Things got tricky when the older **National Basketball Association (NBA)** did not want another team in town competing with the Knicks. The NBA made sure that the armory turned down the ABA.

The ABA solved this problem by placing a team in a temporary home in Teaneck, New Jersey. The club played its first season as the Americans. One year later, they moved to Long Island and became the New York Nets. By the early 1970s, the Nets had a very good team. Led by forward Rick Barry, guard Bill Melchionni, and center Billy Paultz, they reached the **ABA Finals** in the spring of 1972.

Julius Erving joined the Nets for the 1973–74 season. He was a spectacular player who captured the imagination of basketball fans everywhere. With the help of three young stars—John Williamson, Larry Kenon, and Brian Taylor—Erving and the Nets won the ABA Championship. Two years later, Erving led the Nets to a second ABA Championship.

The Nets were one of four clubs invited to join the NBA for the 1976–77 season. When New York traded for superstar Nate Archibald, it looked as if the team would be one of the league's best. Unfortunately, joining the NBA cost much more than team owner Roy Boe expected. He had to let Erving go to the Philadelphia 76ers. New York finished in last place, and few fans came to watch the team play.

The Nets moved to New Jersey prior to the 1977–78 season. They hoped

more people would come to see them in their new home. The team began rebuilding. By the early 1980s, the Nets had a number of good players, including Buck Williams, Otis Birdsong, Albert King, Darryl Dawkins, Mike Gminski, and Micheal Ray Richardson.

LEFT: A program from the early days of the Nets.
ABOVE: This trading card shows Julius Erving's great leaping ability.

During the 1990s, the Nets were led by Derrick Coleman, Jayson Williams, Mookie Blaylock, Drazen Petrovic, and Kenny Anderson. However, the team was not ready to challenge for another championship until the 2001–02 season.

That season, Jason Kidd joined the Nets. The **All-Star** guard helped mold talented players like Kenyon Martin, Kerry Kittles, Richard Jefferson, and Keith Van Horn into an excellent team. The Nets improved to 52 wins and made it all the way to the **NBA Finals**. The following year, the Nets won 49 games and returned to the NBA Finals. Although they lost the championship series both times—to the Los Angeles Lakers and San Antonio Spurs—the Nets were the first team from the **Atlantic Division** to play in the NBA Finals twice in a row since the 1980s.

LEFT: Jason Kidd drives past David Robinson of the San Antonio Spurs during the 2003 NBA Finals.   **ABOVE**: Richard Jefferson dunks the ball.

The Team Today

To most people, the idea of "team basketball" means teammates sharing the ball on offense and helping one another on defense. To the Nets, it means much more. Their goal is to get everyone on the club to think as one, no matter how different their skills may be.

In the NBA, this can be a great challenge. It takes a coach who understands his players and a leader on the court who can "read" his teammates and *inspire* them to be successful. When the Nets have this combination, they do *remarkable* things. When they lack this kind of leadership, they struggle.

The player who set a standard for all future Nets was Jason Kidd. He showed how a point guard could lead a team like a conductor leads an orchestra. In 2008, Devin Harris picked up where Kidd left off. He became the leader of a **roster** that blended **veterans** such as Vince Carter with newcomers like Brook Lopez. By following this successful *formula*, the Nets hope to be a winning team for years to come.

Devin Harris runs up the court as Brook Lopez and Vince Carter slap a high-five during a 2008–09 game.

11

Home Court

The Nets' first home was an armory in Teaneck, New Jersey. They were unable to play their first **postseason game** there because the circus was using the building. When the team found a new location for the game, the court was not ready in time, and they had to *forfeit*.

The Nets played their next nine seasons in Long Island, New York, mostly at the Nassau Coliseum. After moving to New Jersey in 1977, the Nets shared a court with Rutgers University until a new arena was built at the Meadowlands Sports *Complex.* In 2005, the Nets announced plans to move the team to Brooklyn, New York. The site of their new home is a perfect location for fans because it's easy to reach by train, bus, or car.

BY THE NUMBERS

- *The Nets' arena has 20,032 seats for basketball.*
- *The Nets' arena opened in 1981 and hosted the 1982 NBA All-Star Game.*
- *As of 2008–09, the Nets had retired six numbers—3 (Drazen Petrovic), 4 (Wendell Ladner), 23 (John Williamson), 25 (Bill Melchionni), 32 (Julius Erving), and 52 (Buck Williams).*

Yi Jianlian rises high to block a dunk by Dwyane Wade during a 2008–09 game in the Nets' arena.

Dressed for Success

The Nets were originally known as the Americans. They changed their name to the Nets in their second season. It was meant to rhyme with the New York Jets football team and New York Mets baseball team, both of which also started in the 1960s.

The Nets have featured red, white, and blue uniforms every year since the team began playing in the 1967–68 season. They were chosen to match the colors of the ABA ball. The team wore white uniforms at home and blue on the road. In 2006, the Nets introduced a special red uniform. For most of the 1970s and 1980s, they also used stars in their uniform design.

The team's first *logo* featured stars. It showed a stars-and-stripes shield with "N.J. Americans" written across the front. It also had a picture of a basketball. The team has used a basketball *symbol* in its logo almost every season since. When the team played in New York, the lettering in *Nets* helped form a basketball net.

Wendell Ladner wears the Nets uniform of the early 1970s and holds the ABA ball.

UNIFORM BASICS

The basketball uniform is very simple. It consists of a roomy top and baggy shorts.

- The top hangs from the shoulders, with big "scoops" for the arms and neck. This style has not changed much over the years.

- Shorts, however, have changed a lot. They used to be very short, so players could move their legs freely. In the last 20 years, shorts have gotten longer and much baggier.

Basketball uniforms look the same as they did long ago … until you look very closely. In the old days, the shorts had belts and buckles. The tops were made of a thick cotton called "jersey," which got very heavy when players sweated. Later, uniforms were made of shiny *satin*. They may have looked great, but they did not "breathe." As a result, players got very hot! Today, most uniforms are made of *synthetic* materials that soak up sweat and keep the body cool.

Chris Douglas-Roberts shoots a jump shot in the Nets' 2008–09 road uniform.

We Won!

J ulius Erving wore a Nets uniform for three seasons. During those years, the team might have been the best in all of basketball. Erving's first season with the Nets was 1973–74. His teammates included Billy Paultz, Larry Kenon, John Williamson, and Brian Taylor.

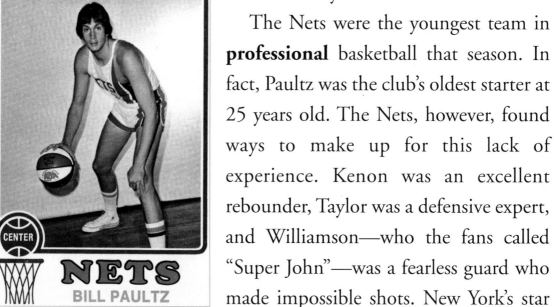

CENTER

NETS
BILL PAULTZ

The Nets were the youngest team in **professional** basketball that season. In fact, Paultz was the club's oldest starter at 25 years old. The Nets, however, found ways to make up for this lack of experience. Kenon was an excellent rebounder, Taylor was a defensive expert, and Williamson—who the fans called "Super John"—was a fearless guard who made impossible shots. New York's star substitute was Wendell Ladner. He loved to dive into the stands to save **loose balls**, and the fans gave him a standing *ovation* every time he did.

Many thought the inexperienced Nets would lose in the **playoffs**. Instead, they showed tremendous *poise*. Coach Kevin Loughery guided them past the Virginia Squires and Kentucky Colonels to reach the ABA Finals. There the Nets met the Utah Stars, who had some of the league's best players.

Erving scored 47 points and played great defense in Game 1, but it was two baskets by Kenon that sealed the team's 89–85 victory. Erving scored 32 points in Game 2, and the Nets won again, 118–94. In Game 3, the Stars looked like they would get their first victory of the series. With the Nets trailing and only 10 seconds left, Ladner tried a wild, off-balance **3-point shot**. When the ball clanked off the rim, Ladner chased down his own rebound and passed quickly to Taylor. He tied the game with a long shot at the buzzer, and the Nets went on to win 103–100 in **overtime**.

After losing Game 4, the Nets finished off the Stars in Game 5. Paultz was the main man in the final game. He scored 21 points, grabbed 12 rebounds, and played great defense.

LEFT: Billy Paultz, who starred in Game 5 of the 1974 ABA Finals.
ABOVE: Julius Erving blocks a shot against the Utah Stars.

Two years later, the Nets returned to the ABA Finals. This time, they played without Paultz and Kenon, who had been traded to the San Antonio Spurs. But Erving, Taylor, and Williamson picked up the slack, along with forward Al Skinner. The Nets beat Paultz, Kenon, and the Spurs in the postseason, and then faced the Denver Nuggets for the ABA Championship.

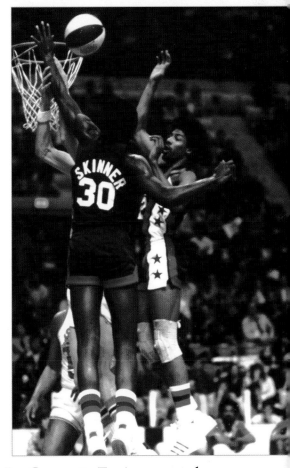

In Game 1, Erving poured in 45 points and hit the winning shot at the buzzer to give New York a 120–118 victory. He followed that performance with 48 points in Game 2, but the Nuggets won 127–121. In Game 3, Erving scored eight points in the final 90 seconds for a 117–111 win.

The Nets won Game 4, but then dropped Game 5. The Nuggets looked like they were on a roll when they went ahead by 22 points late in the third quarter of Game 6. But Williamson caught fire and came to the rescue for the Nets. "Super John" scored 16 points in the final period and led his team to a 112–106 victory. Erving added 31 points and 19 rebounds. The Nets were champions again.

LEFT: Brian Taylor guards George Gervin of the San Antonio Spurs during the 1976 ABA playoffs.
ABOVE: Julius Erving and Al Skinner battle for a rebound.

Go-To Guys

To be a true star in the NBA, you need more than a great shot. You have to be a "go-to guy"—someone teammates trust to make the winning play when the seconds are ticking away in a big game. Nets fans have had a lot to cheer about over the years, including these great stars …

THE PIONEERS

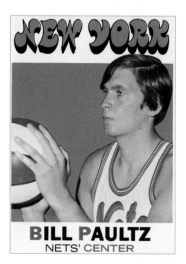

BILL PAULTZ
NETS' CENTER

BILLY PAULTZ   6′ 11″ Center

- BORN: 7/30/1948
- PLAYED FOR TEAM: 1970–71 TO 1974–75

Billy Paultz was a smart center who was difficult to guard. Paultz was nicknamed the "Whopper." Because he was so big and bulky, opponents found him very hard to handle.

RICK BARRY   6′ 7″ Forward

- BORN: 3/28/1944   • PLAYED FOR TEAM: 1970–71 TO 1971–72

Rick Barry was one of the greatest shooters in basketball history, but he was also an excellent passer. Barry scored more than 4,000 points in his two seasons with the Nets and led them to the ABA Finals in the spring of 1972. He was the first Net elected to the **Basketball Hall of Fame**.

ABOVE: Billy Paultz   **RIGHT**: Otis Birdsong

JULIUS ERVING   6′ 7″ Forward

- BORN: 2/22/1950
- PLAYED FOR TEAM: 1973–74 TO 1975–76

Julius Erving was the ABA's most exciting and talented player. "Dr. J" averaged more than 28 points a game with the Nets. Erving was the **Most Valuable Player (MVP)** twice and co-MVP once in his three years with the Nets. He also guided them to two ABA Championships.

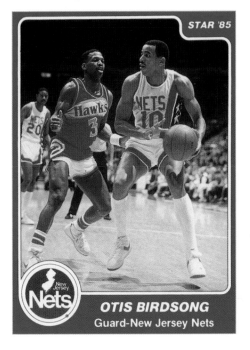

OTIS BIRDSONG   6′ 4″ Guard

- BORN: 12/9/1955
- PLAYED FOR TEAM: 1981–82 TO 1987–88

It is hard to imagine what the Nets would have done without Otis Birdsong in the 1980s. The team reached the playoffs five years in a row after he arrived. Birdsong gave the Nets good scoring, passing, defense, and leadership.

BUCK WILLIAMS   6′ 8″ Forward

- BORN: 3/8/1960
- PLAYED FOR TEAM: 1981–82 TO 1988–89

Buck Williams worked hard at the things that help win basketball games, including rebounding and defense. The year he joined the Nets, they improved by 20 victories. Williams was one of the NBA's top three rebounders six times during the 1980s.

DERRICK COLEMAN   6′ 10″ Forward

• BORN: 6/21/1967 • PLAYED FOR TEAM: 1990–91 TO 1994–95

Derrick Coleman was hard to stop when he got near the basket. He was one of the NBA's top-scoring **power forwards** and one of its best rebounders.

DRAZEN PETROVIC   6′ 5″ Guard

• BORN: 1/22/1964   • DIED: 6/7/1993

• PLAYED FOR TEAM: 1990–91 TO 1992–93

When Drazen Petrovic joined Kenny Anderson and Derrick Coleman on the Nets, he gave the team three up-and-coming stars. The future looked especially bright after "Petro" proved he could score 20 points a game. The team was stunned when he was killed in a car accident at the age of 29.

KENYON MARTIN   6′ 9″ Forward

• BORN: 12/30/1977

• PLAYED FOR TEAM: 2000–01 TO 2003–04

No one on the Nets played harder or more fiercely than Kenyon Martin. He attacked the basket on offense and made opponents work for every shot and rebound. New Jersey reached the NBA Finals in two of Martin's first three seasons.

ABOVE: Drazen Petrovic
TOP RIGHT: Jason Kidd **BOTTOM RIGHT**: Vince Carter

JASON KIDD   6´ 4˝ Guard

- BORN: 3/23/1973
- PLAYED FOR TEAM: 2001–02 TO 2007–08

The Nets took a risk when they traded for Jason Kidd because some people did not believe he was a winner. He proved them wrong by providing great leadership. Kidd's **all-around** game made him the league's most dazzling point guard. Twice he led the Nets to the NBA Finals.

VINCE CARTER   6´ 6˝ Guard/Forward

- BORN: 1/26/1977
- FIRST SEASON WITH TEAM: 2004–05

"Vin-sanity" came to New Jersey when the Nets traded for Vince Carter in 2004. His soaring dunks and acrobatic drives made him the team's most exciting player since Julius Erving.

DEVIN HARRIS   6´ 3˝ Guard

- BORN: 2/27/1983
- FIRST SEASON WITH TEAM: 2007–08

The Nets were thinking about the future when they traded Jason Kidd for Devin Harris in February of 2008. The future came sooner than anyone expected. Harris became one of the top point guards in the NBA.

On the Sidelines

The first coach in team history was a former NBA scoring champion named Max Zaslofsky. Lou Carnesecca took over in 1970 and led the Nets to the ABA Finals in the 1971–72 season.

The Nets won their two ABA Championships under Kevin Loughery. He was a young coach with a short temper. Loughery was smart to hire his friend Rod Thorn as an assistant. Thorn got along well with the players and had a nice way of smoothing things out. Thorn would one day become the team's president.

Since Loughery, the Nets have had several other good coaches, including Larry Brown, Bill Fitch, Chuck Daly, and Byron Scott. It was Scott—who played alongside Magic Johnson on the Los Angeles Lakers in the 1980s—who molded the Nets into championship *contenders*. In 2004, Lawrence Frank became the team's coach and won his first 13 games. No one in the history of basketball, baseball, football, or hockey had ever begun a coaching career with that many victories in a row.

Lawrence Frank sketches out a play for Devin Harris during a 2008–09 game.

One Great Day

Basketball fans got a glimpse of the future during the winter of 1975–76. The ABA and its players would soon become part of the NBA, but the two leagues were quite different. The NBA was known for its rebounding and defense. Many people thought the games were dull. The ABA had creative players who understood the importance of making fans jump out of their seats.

At halftime of the 1976 ABA All-Star Game, a sellout crowd at Denver's McNichols Arena watched the very first Slam Dunk Contest. Millions more tuned in on television. It was one of the few times ABA action could be seen coast-to-coast. Five players lined up to compete: Larry Kenon, George Gervin, Artis Gilmore, David Thompson, and Julius Erving of the Nets. The winner would receive $1,000 and a new stereo.

One of the best dunks of the contest came during warm-ups. Thompson cradled the ball in his elbow, soared above the rim, and punched it down through the hoop with his other hand. Once the competition started, however, Erving took control.

Julius Erving soars above the hoop for his famous dunk at the 1976 ABA All-Star Game.

For his first attempt, "Dr. J" spread his arms like wings, and then dunked the ball behind his head as he flew past the hoop. For his second attempt, he started from beneath the basket with a ball in each hand and slammed one down right after the other. On Erving's third dunk, he jumped under the backboard, grabbed the rim with his right hand, and swung around to jam with his left.

The fans and players were going crazy. They were all waiting to see what Erving's final dunk would be. He walked past halfcourt, turned toward the basket, took a deep breath, and started running toward the hoop. The arena was so quiet that each squeak of his sneakers could be heard. Erving's final step came just at the foul line. He took off, rose toward the rim, and threw the ball down through the net as the crowd erupted in cheers. Erving was the winner—no one else even came close.

Legend Has It

Which team was whistled for eight technical fouls on one play?

LEGEND HAS IT that the Nets were. In a 1976 game against the Virginia Squires, coach Kevin Loughery believed the Squires were playing a **zone defense**, which was illegal. When the referees did not see it his way, Loughery ordered the Nets to play a zone defense of their own in protest. When the referees stopped the game, Loughery and his players began arguing. Eight **technical fouls** were called before order was restored.

Kevin Loughery gives the Nets a pep talk.

Were the Nets almost called the Freighters?

LEGEND HAS IT that they were. Their first owner, Arthur Brown, owned a gigantic fleet of trucks that moved freight all over the United States. He thought calling his team the Freighters would be good for his business. Brown changed his mind before the season started and decided on Americans. A year later, the team became the Nets.

Has a player ever worn both teams' uniforms in the same game?

LEGEND HAS IT that three have. During the 1978–79 season, the Nets lost a game to the Philadelphia 76ers by a score of 137–133. The NBA later realized the referees had made a mistake in the third quarter. The league ordered the game to be replayed from that point—several months later! Before the replay, however, the Nets and 76ers made a trade. Ralph Simpson and Harvey Catchings—who were 76ers at the start of the game—would finish the game as members of the Nets. Eric Money, who began the game as a Net, would finish it as a 76er. All three players appeared in the official scoresheet for both teams.

It Really Happened

T he Nets have played some close games over the years. However, no game was closer—or more exciting—than their playoff battle with the Indiana Pacers on May 2nd, 2002.

It had been nearly two **decades** since the Nets had won a series in the playoffs. This game against Indiana was do-or-die. The teams were tied at two wins each in their best-of-five series. The winner would keep playing, and the loser would go home for the summer.

The Nets had fire in their eyes to start the game. No player was more focused than Kenyon Martin. His teammate Jason Kidd had challenged him the day before to raise his game. Martin responded with an amazing effort.

The only problem for the Nets was that Indiana was equally intense. Every time New Jersey took a lead, the Pacers fought back.

The teams were tied at halftime and at the end of the third quarter. Then, with the Nets up by three points in the final period, Indiana's Reggie Miller banked a 39-foot shot off the backboard at the buzzer to tie the game at 96–96.

In overtime, the Pacers went ahead, but Kidd brought the Nets back. He made two baskets and then passed to Martin for a dunk. The game moved into a second overtime period.

New Jersey refused to lose. Kidd hit a jumper with two minutes left to give the Nets the lead, and they finally pulled away to win 120–109. Kidd finished with 31 points. Martin, who played 56 minutes, scored 29. The two hugged each other after the game ended.

"We stuck it out and it showed how bad we wanted it," said Martin. "We want to keep going. We don't want to stop here."

The Nets did not stop there. They beat the Charlotte Hornets and then the Boston Celtics in the **Eastern Conference Finals** to make it to the NBA Finals for the first time in team history.

LEFT: Kenyon Martin dunks against the Pacers.   **ABOVE**: Jason Kidd hears the cheers from the crowd after the win over Indiana.

Team Spirit

The Nets made a lot of new fans after reaching the NBA Finals in 2002 and 2003. Their attacking style and unselfish play sparked interest in the team all over the New York–New Jersey metropolitan area. Their success was especially rewarding to their old-time fans. Some had been rooting for the team since it was the New Jersey Americans!

One of the Nets' biggest supporters is Shawn Corey Carter, who is better known as hip-hop star Jay–Z. In 2004, he actually purchased part of the team. Since then, some of the biggest names in the music business have watched the Nets from his courtside seats.

After three decades in New Jersey, the Nets announced that they would be going "back to the future." The team plans to move to New York and play in a new arena in Brooklyn. It will mean a longer drive for many fans in New Jersey, but thousands who could not get to the Meadowlands will be just a subway ride away.

Jay-Z watches the action courtside at a Nets game with Beyoncé Knowles.

Timeline

The basketball season is played from October through June. That means each season takes place at the end of one year and halfway through the next. In this timeline, the accomplishments of the Nets are shown by season.

1967–68
The team plays its first season as the New Jersey Americans.

1975–76
The Nets win their second ABA Championship.

1971–72
Bill Melchionni leads the ABA in **assists**.

1973–74
The Nets win their first ABA Championship.

1976–77
The Nets join the NBA.

BILL MELCHIONNI
NETS' GUARD

Bill Melchionni

The 1973–74 Nets

NEW YORK NETS

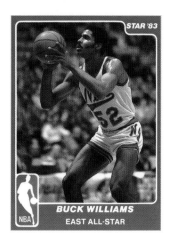

Buck
Williams

A pennant from the 2002–03 playoffs.

1984–85
Buck Williams leads the NBA in minutes played.

1990–91
Derrick Coleman is named NBA **Rookie of the Year**.

2002–03
The Nets reach the NBA Finals for the second time.

1977–78
The Nets move to New Jersey.

2001–02
The Nets reach the NBA Finals for the first time.

2008–09
Devin Harris is named to the All-Star Game.

Kenyon Martin dunks against the Los Angeles Lakers in the 2002 NBA Finals.

Fun Facts

SWAT TEAM

The 1977–78 Nets did not win many games, but no team in the NBA blocked more shots. New Jersey had 560 blocks in all. The team's center, George Johnson, led the league with 274.

1st TEAM
★ ABA ALL-STARS
'71-72 Rick BARRY
New York Nets • Forward

KEEP IT SIMPLE

The best free throw shooter in Nets history was Rick Barry. He was famous for taking his foul shots underhand.

DOING THE IMPOSSIBLE

During the 1983–84 season, coach Stan Albeck guaranteed that the Nets would make the playoffs and win their first series. When the season ended, the Nets found themselves paired with the defending NBA champion Philadelphia 76ers. Incredibly, the Nets won the series, winning all three of their games on Philadelphia's home court!

ABOVE: Rick Barry   **RIGHT**: Vince Carter

PLAYING DOCTOR

Vince Carter grew up *idolizing* Julius Erving. Carter made his first dunk at age 12. In high school, he won a dunking contest using Erving's famous foul-line jam.

EASTERN BLOCK

Each year from 2002 to 2004, the Nets chose a young Eastern European star with their first pick in the **NBA draft**—Nenad Krstic (Serbia), Zoran Planinic (Croatia), and Viktor Khryapa (Russia).

SWAMP THINGS

After several losing seasons during the 1990s, the Nets wondered if changing their name might change their luck. They decided not to. The leading choice at the time was "Swamp Dragons."

Talking Hoops

"Passing is ***contagious***. There's nothing better than making the pass that gives someone an easy hoop."
—Jason Kidd, on the rewards of being an unselfish player

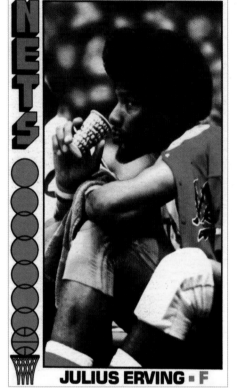

JULIUS ERVING · F

"When the crowd appreciates you, it encourages you to be a little more daring."
—Julius Erving, on the energy he felt from Nets fans

"The **merger agreement** got us into the NBA, but it forced me to destroy the team by selling Erving to pay the bill."
—Roy Boe, on losing Julius Erving in 1976–77

"We wanted to win one for Julius, because if that was going to be the last year of the ABA, Julius deserved to be on the last championship team."
—Kevin Loughery, on the motivation for the Nets to win the 1975–76 ABA title

38

"I just try to be me, and just try to play the way I know I can."
—*Devin Harris on "filling the shoes" of Jason Kidd as leader of the Nets*

"It's the only style we know how to play—the unselfish, teammate-first brand of basketball that characterizes the New Jersey Nets."
—*Lawrence Frank, on following in the footsteps of other great Nets teams*

"If your mind rules, your game rules."
—*Kenyon Martin, on the mental side of basketball*

LEFT: Julius Erving
ABOVE: Jason Kidd and Devin Harris

For the Record

T he great Nets teams and players have left their marks on the record books. These are the "best of the best" …

Brian Taylor

NETS AWARD WINNERS

WINNER	AWARD	SEASON
Brian Taylor	ABA Rookie of the Year	1972–73
Julius Erving	ABA Most Valuable Player	1973–74
Julius Erving	ABA Finals MVP	1973–74
Julius Erving	ABA co-Most Valuable Player	1974–75
Julius Erving	ABA Slam Dunk Champion	1975–76
Julius Erving	ABA Most Valuable Player	1975–76
Julius Erving	ABA Finals MVP	1975–76
Buck Williams	NBA Rookie of the Year	1981–82
Derrick Coleman	NBA Rookie of the Year	1990–91

Derrick Coleman

Buck Williams smiles during the ceremony to retire his number.

NETS ACHIEVEMENTS

ACHIEVEMENT	SEASON
ABA Eastern Division Champions	1973–74
ABA Champions	1973–74
ABA Champions	1975–76
Atlantic Division Champions	2001–02
Eastern Conference Champions	2001–02
Atlantic Division Champions	2002–03
Eastern Conference Champions	2002–03
Atlantic Division Champions	2003–04
Atlantic Division Champions	2005–06

KENYON
MARTIN
FORWARD

JOHN WILLIAMSON ▪ G

RICHARD
JEFFERSON
FORWARD-GUARD

LEFT: John Williamson, a hero on the 1974 and 1976 championship teams.
ABOVE: Kenyon Martin and Richard Jefferson, who helped the Nets reach the NBA Finals in 2002 and 2003.

Pinpoints

The history of a basketball team is made up of many smaller stories. These stories take place all over the map—not just in the city a team calls "home." Match the pushpins on these maps to the Team Facts and you will begin to see the story of the Nets unfold!

TEAM FACTS

1 East Rutherford, New Jersey—*The Nets began playing here in 1981.*
2 Uniondale, New York—*The Nets played here from 1972 to 1977.*
3 Rocky Mount, North Carolina—*Buck Williams was born here.*
4 Orlando, Florida—*Darryl Dawkins was born here.*
5 Birmingham, Alabama—*Larry Kenon was born here.*
6 Necaise Crossing, Mississippi—*Wendell Ladner was born here.*
7 Garland, Texas—*Mookie Blaylock was born here.*
8 Saginaw, Michigan—*Kenyon Martin was born here.*
9 San Francisco, California—*Jason Kidd was born here.*
10 Los Angeles, California—*Richard Jefferson was born here.*
11 Sibenik, Croatia—*Drazen Petrovic was born here.*
12 Guangdong, China—*Yi Jianlian was born here.*

Darryl Dawkins

Play Ball

Basketball is a sport played by two teams of five players. NBA games have four 12-minute quarters—48 minutes in all—and the team that scores the most points when time has run out is the winner. Most baskets count for two points. Players who make shots from beyond the 3-point line receive an extra point. Baskets made from the free-throw line count for one point. Free throws are penalty shots awarded to a team, usually after an opponent has committed a foul. A foul is called when one player makes hard contact with another.

Players can move around all they want, but the player with the ball cannot. He must bounce the ball with one hand or the other (but never both) in order to go from one part of the court to another. As long as he keeps "dribbling," he can keep moving.

In the NBA, teams must attempt a shot within 24 seconds, so there is little time to waste. The job of the defense is to make it as difficult as possible for the offense to take a good shot—and to grab the ball if the other team shoots and misses.

This may sound simple, but anyone who has played the game knows that basketball can be very complicated. Every player on the court has a job to do. Different players have different strengths and weaknesses. The coach must mix these players in just the right way and teach them to work together as one.

The more you play and watch basketball, the more "little things" you are likely to notice. The next time you watch a game, look for these plays:

PLAY LIST

ALLEY-OOP—A play in which the passer throws the ball just to the side of the rim—so a teammate can catch it and dunk in one motion.

BACK-DOOR PLAY—A play in which the passer waits for a teammate to fake the defender away from the basket—then throws him the ball when he cuts back toward the basket.

KICK-OUT—A play in which the ball handler waits for the defense to surround him—then quickly passes to a teammate who is open for an outside shot. The ball is not really kicked in this play; the term comes from the action of pinball machines.

NO-LOOK PASS—A play in which a passer fools the defense by looking in one direction, then making a surprise pass to a teammate in another direction.

PICK-AND-ROLL—A play in which one player blocks, or "picks off," a teammate's defender with his body, then in the confusion cuts to the basket for a pass.

Glossary

BASKETBALL WORDS TO KNOW

3-POINT SHOT—A shot attempted from behind the 3-point line.

ABA FINALS—The series that decided the ABA champion.

ALL-AROUND—Good at all parts of the game.

ALL-STAR—Describing a player selected to play in the annual All-Star Game.

AMERICAN BASKETBALL ASSOCIATION (ABA)—The basketball league that played for nine seasons starting in 1967. Prior to the 1976–77 season four ABA teams joined the NBA, and the rest went out of business.

ASSISTS—Passes that lead to successful shots.

ATLANTIC DIVISION—A group of teams that play in a region that is close to the Atlantic Ocean.

BASKETBALL HALL OF FAME—The museum in Springfield, Massachusetts where basketball's greatest players are honored. A player voted into the Hall of Fame is sometimes called a "Hall of Famer."

EASTERN CONFERENCE FINALS—The playoff series that determines which team from the East will play the best team from the West for the NBA Championship.

LOOSE BALLS—Balls that are not controlled by either team.

MERGER AGREEMENT—A business deal to combine two leagues. The ABA and NBA merged in 1976.

MOST VALUABLE PLAYER (MVP)—The award given each year to the league's best player; also given to the best player in the league finals and All-Star Game.

NATIONAL BASKETBALL ASSOCIATION (NBA)—The professional league that has been operating since 1946–47.

NBA DRAFT—The annual meeting where teams pick from a group of the best college players.

NBA FINALS—The playoff series that decides the champion of the league.

OVERTIME—The extra period played when a game is tied after 48 minutes.

PLAYOFFS—The games played after the season to determine the league champion.

POSTSEASON GAME—A game played after the regular season to determine the league champion.

POWER FORWARDS—The bigger and stronger of a team's forwards.

PROFESSIONAL—A player or team that plays a sport for money.

ROOKIE OF THE YEAR—The annual award given to the league's best first-year player.

ROSTER—The list of players on a team.

SUBSTITUTES—Players who begin most games on the bench.

TECHNICAL FOULS—Fouls called on a player or coach for arguing with a referee or showing bad sportsmanship.

VETERANS—Players with great experience.

ZONE DEFENSE—A defense in which players are responsible for guarding an area of the court rather than covering a specific offensive player.

OTHER WORDS TO KNOW

ARMORY—A spacious building where military equipment is stored.

COMPLEX—A series of buildings grouped together.

CONTAGIOUS—Causing similar feelings in others.

CONTENDERS—People who compete for a championship.

DECADES—Periods of 10 years; also specific periods, such as the 1950s.

FORFEIT—Lose a game because of a rules violation.

FORMULA—A set way of doing something.

IDOLIZING—Admiring greatly.

INSPIRE—Give positive and confident feelings to others.

LOGO—A symbol or design that represents a company or team.

OVATION—A long, loud cheer.

POISE—Calm and confident.

REMARKABLE—Unusual or exceptional.

SATIN—A smooth, shiny fabric.

SYMBOL—Something that represents a thought or idea.

SYNTHETIC—Made in a laboratory, not in nature.

UPBEAT—Cheerful and confident about the future.

Places to Go

ON THE ROAD

NEW JERSEY NETS
50 Route 120
East Rutherford, New Jersey 07073
(201) 935-8888

NAISMITH MEMORIAL BASKETBALL HALL OF FAME
1000 West Columbus Avenue
Springfield, Massachusetts 01105
(877) 4HOOPLA

ON THE WEB

THE NATIONAL BASKETBALL ASSOCIATION   www.nba.com
  • *Learn more about the league's teams, players, and history*

THE NEW JERSEY NETS   www.njnets.com
  • *Learn more about the New Jersey Nets*

THE BASKETBALL HALL OF FAME   www.hoophall.com
  • *Learn more about history's greatest players*

ON THE BOOKSHELF

To learn more about the sport of basketball, look for these books at your library or bookstore:
  • Stewart, Mark and Kennedy, Mike. *Swish: the Quest for Basketball's Perfect Shot.* Minneapolis, Minnesota: Millbrook Press, 2009.
  • Ramen, Fred. *Basketball: Rules, Tips, Strategy & Safety.* New York, New York: Rosen Central, 2007.
  • Labrecque, Ellen. *Basketball.* Ann Arbor, Michigan: Cherry Lake Publishing, 2009.
  • Wyckoff, Edwin Brit. *The Man Who Invented Basketball: James Naismith and His Amazing Game.* Berkeley Heights, New Jersey: Enslow Elementary, 2008.

Index

The Team

MARK STEWART has written more than 20 books on basketball, and over 100 sports books for kids. He grew up in New York City during the 1960s rooting for the Knicks and Nets, and now takes his two daughters, Mariah and Rachel, to watch them play. Mark comes from a family of writers. His grandfather was Sunday Editor of *The New York Times* and his mother was Articles Editor of *The Ladies Home Journal* and *McCall's*. Mark has profiled hundreds of athletes over the last 20 years. He has also written several books about his native New York, and New Jersey, his home today. Mark is a graduate of Duke University, with a degree in history. He lives with his daughters and wife, Sarah, overlooking Sandy Hook, New Jersey.

MATT ZEYSING is the resident historian at the Basketball Hall of Fame in Springfield, Massachusetts. His research interests include the origins of the game of basketball, the development of professional basketball in the first half of the 20th century, and the culture and meaning of basketball in American society.